I0454342

Anti-inflammatory Diets basic

to advance cookbook

The simple and easy Meal Plan and
100+ Recipes to Simplify Your
Healing

By

Janet Ryles

Table of contents

- Turmeric and its potent anti-inflammatory compound, curcumin
- Harnessing the benefits of ginger, garlic, and other flavorful additions

4. Heart-Healthy Fats: Omega-3s and Beyond
   - Incorporating omega-3-rich foods like fatty fish and flaxseeds
   - Choosing healthy fats for cooking and meal preparation

5. Seafood Specialties From the Sea to the Plate
   - Delicious recipes featuring salmon, mackerel, and other anti-inflammatory fish

- Mastering cooking methods that preserve nutritional value
- Elevating flavors with advanced culinary skills

9. Balancing Act: Crafting Well-Balanced Anti-Inflammatory Meals
   - Designing meals that combine proteins, fats, and carbohydrates effectively
   - Portion control and mindful eating for inflammation management

10. Sweet Endings: Desserts with a Health Twist
    - Indulging in treats without compromising anti-inflammatory principles

This cookbook serves as a comprehensive guide, from the basics of anti-inflammatory eating to advanced culinary techniques, ensuring a flavorful and health-enhancing culinary experience.

Introduction

Welcome to the journey of vibrant health and well-being! In "Anti-Inflammatory Diets: Basic to Advanced Cookbook," we embark on a culinary exploration designed to nourish your body and soothe inflammation from its roots. This cookbook is not just a collection of recipes; it's a guide to transforming your relationship with food.

Discover a symphony of flavors as we navigate the realm of nutrient-dense ingredients, from luscious berries to hearty greens. Uncover the power of anti-inflammatory superfoods, and learn to weave them into your daily culinary tapestry. Whether you're a kitchen novice or a seasoned chef, our recipes cater to all skill levels, making the transition to an anti-inflammatory lifestyle effortlessly delicious.

Embrace the healing potential of spices like turmeric and ginger, dance with the omega-3 richness of salmon, and savor the wholesome goodness of whole grains. Each recipe is a step towards cultivating a balanced, inflammation-free life. With a bounty of options spanning from the basic foundations to advanced gastronomic delights, this cookbook empowers you to craft meals that not only delight your taste buds but also nurture your body.

Let this cookbook be your compass on the path to vitality, providing you with the knowledge and inspiration to create meals that are both satisfying and healing. Say goodbye to inflammation, and welcome a vibrant, flavorful chapter of wellness into your life. Your path to better health begins here.

Chapter One

Introduction to Anti-Inflammatory Diets

Welcome to the transformative journey of "Anti-Inflammatory Diets: Basic to Advanced Cookbook." In this opening chapter, we delve into the fundamental understanding of inflammation and its profound impact on our overall health. Let's embark on a quest to unravel the principles that underpin the anti-inflammatory diet, setting the stage for a culinary adventure that nourishes both body and soul.

Understanding Inflammation: A Holistic Perspective

Inflammation, while a natural response to injury or infection, can become chronic and detrimental to our health. We explore the mechanisms behind inflammation, shedding light on how dietary choices play a pivotal role in either fueling or mitigating this process. By grasping the basics, readers gain insights into the importance of adopting an anti-inflammatory lifestyle.

Overview of the Anti-Inflammatory Diet Approach

This section provides a roadmap for navigating the anti-inflammatory landscape. We outline key principles, emphasizing the consumption of whole, nutrient-dense foods while minimizing processed and inflammatory-inducing choices. The chapter acts as a guide, ensuring readers understand the core philosophy that will be woven into each recipe throughout the cookbook.

Benefits of Anti-Inflammatory Eating: Beyond the Plate

Delving into the advantages of an anti-inflammatory diet extends beyond managing inflammation. We explore how this dietary approach positively influences various aspects of health, from cardiovascular well-being to cognitive function. By understanding the broader benefits, readers are motivated to embrace anti-inflammatory eating not just as a culinary choice but as a lifestyle.

Making Informed Choices: Navigating the Dietary Landscape

The chapter equips readers with practical knowledge for making informed dietary choices. We discuss label reading, identifying inflammatory culprits, and discerning between wholesome and processed foods. This section empowers individuals to navigate grocery store aisles with confidence, ensuring they select ingredients that align with the anti-inflammatory principles outlined in the cookbook.

Setting the Tone: Cultivating a Mindful Approach to Eating

Recognizing the interconnectedness of mind and body, we introduce the concept of mindful eating. From savoring flavors to paying attention to hunger and fullness cues, this section emphasizes the importance of cultivating a positive relationship with food. Mindful eating becomes a cornerstone of anti-inflammatory living, fostering a holistic approach to well-being.

By the end of Chapter 1, readers are not only introduced to the core tenets of anti-inflammatory diets but are also inspired to embark on a journey that transcends mere culinary exploration. This chapter lays the foundation for the chapters to come, creating a holistic understanding of how the choices we make in the kitchen can profoundly impact our health and vitality.

Chapter Two

Building a Foundation - Essential Ingredients

In this pivotal chapter, we embark on a culinary exploration of the essential ingredients that form the foundation of an anti-inflammatory diet. From vibrant fruits and vegetables to whole grains and lean proteins, we uncover the nutritional powerhouses that will redefine the way we nourish our bodies.

Exploring Nutrient-Dense Fruits and Vegetables

The journey begins with an exploration of the colorful world of fruits and vegetables. We delve into the nutritional richness of leafy greens, cruciferous vegetables, and a spectrum of antioxidant-packed berries. Readers discover how these plant-based wonders not only contribute to a visually appealing plate but also provide a diverse array of vitamins, minerals, and phytonutrients crucial for combating inflammation.

Whole Grains: A Cornerstone of Anti-Inflammatory Eating

This section is a celebration of whole grains as a cornerstone in crafting wholesome, anti-inflammatory meals. From the nutty goodness of quinoa to the earthy embrace of farro, we showcase a variety of grains that offer not only robust flavors but also a wealth of fiber and essential nutrients. Through recipes and cooking tips, readers gain the confidence to incorporate these grains into their daily repertoire.

Lean Proteins and Their Role in Reducing Inflammation

Protein is an essential component of any diet, and here we focus on lean sources that align with anti-inflammatory principles. From poultry to plant-based proteins like legumes and tofu, we explore options that not only satisfy the palate but also support muscle health and reduce inflammation. The chapter emphasizes the balance between various protein sources for a well-rounded and nourishing diet.

Creating Flavorful Combinations: Culinary Alchemy

Guiding readers beyond individual ingredients, this section explores the art of combining flavors to create culinary masterpieces. We provide practical tips for enhancing dishes with herbs, spices, and seasonings known for their anti-inflammatory properties. The chapter acts as a bridge, connecting the individual components discussed earlier into cohesive, delicious meals that inspire a lifelong love for anti-inflammatory cooking.

Recipes that Inspire: Putting Knowledge into Practice

The chapter concludes with a selection of beginner-friendly recipes that showcase the synergy of essential anti-inflammatory ingredients. From refreshing salads to satisfying main courses, these recipes serve as a practical guide for readers to embark on their culinary journey. Each recipe is crafted to not only tantalize taste buds but also deliver a nutritional punch, making anti-inflammatory eating an accessible and enjoyable endeavor.

As we navigate through Chapter 2, readers gain a profound understanding of the key ingredients that lay the groundwork for an anti-inflammatory lifestyle. Armed with knowledge and culinary inspiration, they are ready to venture into the subsequent chapters, where these foundational elements will be woven into a tapestry of vibrant, inflammation-fighting meals.

Chapter Three

Spice it Up - Culinary Power of Anti-Inflammatory Herbs and Spices

Welcome to a sensory journey through Chapter 3, where we unlock the vibrant world of herbs and spices known for their potent anti-inflammatory properties. Beyond adding flavor, these culinary gems play a pivotal role in elevating our meals to a new level of wellness.

Turmeric and its Potent Anti-Inflammatory Compound, Curcumin

The chapter begins with the golden spice, turmeric, celebrated for its active compound, curcumin. We delve into the science behind curcumin's anti-inflammatory effects, exploring its potential to reduce inflammation at a molecular level. Readers discover creative ways to incorporate turmeric into their cooking, from aromatic curries to soothing turmeric-infused beverages.

Harnessing the Benefits of Ginger, Garlic, and Other Flavorful Additions

As we journey beyond turmeric, the spotlight turns to ginger and garlic, both renowned for their anti-inflammatory and immune-boosting properties. We explore their culinary versatility, from zesty marinades to comforting teas. The chapter extends to an array of flavorful additions such as cinnamon, cayenne, and cilantro, each contributing not only to taste but also to the overall anti-inflammatory profile of our meals.

Creative Uses in Everyday Cooking: Practical Tips

This section is a hands-on guide, offering practical tips on incorporating anti-inflammatory herbs and spices into everyday cooking. Whether it's infusing oils, creating spice blends, or experimenting with fresh herbs, readers gain insights into how small, intentional additions can transform ordinary dishes into anti-inflammatory delights.

Recipes That Showcase Spice Harmony

Chapter 3 culminates in a collection of recipes designed to showcase the harmonious interplay of anti-inflammatory herbs and spices. From tantalizing turmeric-infused soups to garlic and ginger-infused stir-fries, these recipes are a testament to the versatility of anti-inflammatory cooking. Each dish not only promises a culinary adventure but also delivers a nutritional punch, ensuring that flavor and well-being go hand in hand.

Culinary Creativity Unleashed: Beyond the Basics

The chapter concludes by encouraging readers to unleash their culinary creativity. We explore advanced uses of herbs and spices, inspiring individuals to experiment with flavors, textures, and aromatic profiles. By the end of Chapter 3, readers not only grasp the science behind anti-inflammatory herbs and spices but also feel empowered to infuse their kitchens with the transformative power of these culinary treasures.

As we turn the pages of this chapter, we embark on a fragrant and flavorful journey, discovering that the path to anti-inflammatory eating is as rich and diverse as the spices that grace our kitchens. Chapter 3 is a celebration of culinary artistry, inviting readers to embrace the healing potential of herbs and spices with every delicious bite.

Chapter Four

Heart-Healthy Fats - Omega-3s and Beyond

Welcome to a chapter that unravels the wonders of heart-healthy fats, a cornerstone of anti-inflammatory diets. Here, we explore the essential role of omega-3 fatty acids and delve into a diverse world of fats that not only satiate our taste buds but also nourish our bodies for optimal well-being.

Incorporating Omega-3 Rich Foods: Fatty Fish and Flaxseeds

We begin with a deep dive into omega-3 fatty acids, emphasizing the benefits of including fatty fish like salmon, mackerel, and sardines in our diet. These marine treasures are not only delicious but also renowned for their anti-inflammatory and cardiovascular benefits. Additionally, we explore plant-based sources of omega-3s, such as flaxseeds and chia seeds, offering options for individuals following vegetarian or vegan dietary preferences.

Choosing Healthy Fats for Cooking and Meal Preparation

Navigating beyond omega-3s, this section guides readers in selecting healthy fats for cooking. We discuss the merits of olive oil, avocado oil, and other plant-based oils rich in monounsaturated fats, which contribute to heart health and possess anti-inflammatory properties. Practical tips for incorporating these fats into daily meal preparation add a culinary dimension to the chapter.

Balancing Fats in the Diet: A Holistic Approach

The chapter emphasizes the importance of balance when it comes to fats. By understanding the distinction between healthy and unhealthy fats, readers gain insights into crafting meals that promote inflammation reduction. We explore the concept of a well-balanced diet, ensuring that fats play a harmonious role alongside proteins, carbohydrates, and a myriad of anti-inflammatory ingredients.

Navigating Sustainable Seafood: Ethical and Health Considerations

Recognizing the importance of sustainability, this section provides guidance on choosing seafood responsibly. We discuss the environmental impact of fishing practices and provide tips for selecting sustainably sourced seafood, aligning with principles that not only promote personal health but also contribute to the health of our planet.

Recipes that Celebrate Healthy Fats: From Ocean to Plate

Chapter 4 culminates in a collection of recipes that celebrate the richness of heart-healthy fats. From omega-3-rich grilled salmon to avocado-infused salads, these recipes showcase the versatility of incorporating healthy fats into every meal. Each dish not only delights the palate but also delivers essential nutrients for supporting a well-functioning, anti-inflammatory system.

As we conclude this chapter, readers are equipped with a comprehensive understanding of the vital role that heart-healthy fats play in an anti-inflammatory lifestyle. From oceanic delights to plant-based treasures, the world of healthy fats unfolds as a culinary adventure, inviting individuals to savor the goodness of fats that nourish the body and protect against inflammation.

Chapter Five

From the Sea to the Plate - Seafood Specialties

In this captivating chapter, we embark on a culinary exploration of seafood, uncovering its unique flavors, nutritional benefits, and its role as a cornerstone in anti-inflammatory diets. Join us as we navigate the waters of sustainable choices, omega-3 richness, and the art of transforming sea treasures into delectable dishes.

Delicious Recipes Featuring Salmon, Mackerel, and More

The journey begins with an exploration of seafood superstars like salmon, known for its omega-3 richness, and mackerel, celebrated for its distinct flavor profile. Through a series of enticing recipes, readers are guided on how to prepare these oceanic delights, ensuring a harmonious balance between taste and anti-inflammatory nutrition.

Tips for Sourcing Sustainable Seafood

Sustainability takes center stage as we navigate the considerations of ethical and responsible seafood consumption. This section provides practical tips for selecting and sourcing seafood that aligns with environmentally conscious practices. By making informed choices, readers contribute not only to their own health but also to the health of our oceans.

Diverse Seafood Options: Beyond the Basics

Beyond the familiar, this section introduces readers to a diverse array of seafood options, from nutrient-dense shellfish to lesser-known varieties rich in essential minerals and omega-3 fatty acids. Through engaging narratives and recipes, readers are encouraged to broaden their seafood palate, discovering new tastes while reaping the anti-inflammatory benefits.

Creative Seafood Cooking Techniques: Unlocking Flavors

The chapter unfolds with a focus on creative cooking techniques that accentuate the natural flavors of seafood. Grilling, baking, and poaching take center stage as we explore methods that preserve the nutritional integrity of seafood while infusing it with aromatic profiles that elevate each dish to a culinary masterpiece.

The Art of Pairing: Complementing Seafood with Anti-Inflammatory Ingredients

This section is a symphony of flavors, guiding readers in pairing seafood with complementary anti-inflammatory ingredients. From citrus-infused marinades to herb-laden accompaniments, each recipe is crafted to not only showcase the delicate flavors of seafood but also maximize its potential in reducing inflammation.

Savoring the Ocean's Bounty: Culinary Delights Await

As we conclude this chapter, readers find themselves immersed in the world of seafood specialties, armed with the knowledge and inspiration to make seafood a central element of their anti-inflammatory journey. From the ocean to the plate, this chapter celebrates the delights of seafood while emphasizing the profound impact it can have on promoting health and well-being.

Chapter Six

Plant-Based Wonders - Vegetarian and Vegan Delights

In this chapter, we embark on a vibrant journey through plant-based culinary landscapes, celebrating the richness of vegetarian and vegan options that not only tantalize the taste buds but also serve as pillars in an anti-inflammatory diet. Join us as we explore the diverse world of plant-powered nourishment.

Exploring Plant-Based Proteins for a Meatless Approach

The chapter begins by unraveling the variety of plant-based proteins that form the backbone of meatless anti-inflammatory meals. From legumes like lentils and chickpeas to protein-packed tofu and tempeh, readers are introduced to a spectrum of options that deliver essential nutrients while promoting a diet centered around plants.

Creating Satisfying and Nutritionally Balanced Vegetarian Meals

Through a lens of culinary creativity, we delve into the art of crafting vegetarian meals that are not only satisfying but also nutritionally balanced. The chapter provides insights into combining different plant-based elements to ensure a harmonious blend of proteins, carbohydrates, and fats, fostering meals that stand as testament to the delicious possibilities of meat-free eating.

Embracing the Power of Whole Foods: Vegetables, Grains, and More

Beyond plant-based proteins, we explore the inherent goodness of whole foods, emphasizing the role of vegetables, whole grains, nuts, and seeds in creating diverse and nourishing vegetarian and vegan dishes. The chapter advocates for a holistic approach to plant-based eating, encouraging readers to embrace a spectrum of colorful, nutrient-dense ingredients.

Adventurous Cooking with Plant-Based Ingredients: Flavorful Discoveries

As we journey further, the chapter unfolds into an exploration of adventurous cooking techniques with plant-based ingredients. From spiralizing vegetables for vibrant noodle alternatives to experimenting with plant-based cheese and non-dairy milk, readers are invited to push culinary boundaries and discover the limitless possibilities of meatless cooking.

Balancing Nutrients in Plant-Based Diets: Practical Tips

Recognizing the importance of balanced nutrition in plant-based diets, this section offers practical tips for ensuring adequate intake of essential nutrients such as protein, iron, calcium, and B vitamins. Readers gain valuable insights into creating well-rounded meals that not only satisfy taste cravings but also support overall health.

Recipes that Inspire: Culinary Artistry with Plants

The chapter culminates in a collection of inspired recipes that showcase the versatility of plant-based ingredients. From hearty lentil stews to refreshing quinoa salads, each recipe is a celebration of plant-powered goodness, demonstrating that an anti-inflammatory diet can be both delicious and deeply satisfying without the need for animal products.

As we conclude this chapter, readers are equipped with the tools to embrace the vibrant world of plant-based wonders, understanding that meatless meals can be both nourishing and exciting. This exploration of vegetarian and vegan delights stands as a testament to the richness of plant-based eating in the context of anti-inflammatory living.

Chapter Seven

Whole Grains Unveiled - Beyond Brown Rice

Welcome to a chapter that takes a deep dive into the diverse and wholesome world of whole grains, showcasing their versatility and nutritional richness. From quinoa to farro, this chapter unveils the delicious potential of whole grains, proving that they are not just a side dish but can take center stage in anti-inflammatory cooking.

Diving into Diverse Whole Grains: A Culinary Adventure

The chapter commences by introducing readers to a spectrum of whole grains that extend far beyond the familiar brown rice. We explore the nutty nuances of quinoa, the chewy texture of farro, and the robust flavor of bulgur, guiding readers to venture beyond the ordinary and embrace the diverse array of grains that contribute to a well-rounded, anti-inflammatory diet.

Creative Recipes Showcasing Quinoa, Farro, and More

Building on this foundation, the chapter unfolds into a collection of creative recipes that highlight the unique qualities of various whole grains. From quinoa salads bursting with colors to hearty farro bowls brimming with flavor, each recipe is a testament to the culinary artistry that can be achieved by incorporating diverse whole grains into everyday meals.

Cooking Techniques for Whole Grain Excellence

Beyond recipes, the chapter offers insights into cooking techniques that elevate whole grains to new heights. From pilaf-style preparations to risottos and grain bowls, readers are guided on how to coax out the best flavors and textures from different grains. Practical tips for soaking, sprouting, and cooking times empower individuals to confidently experiment with whole grains in their culinary endeavors.

The Nutritional Power of Whole Grains: A Healthful Approach

Delving deeper, we explore the nutritional powerhouse that whole grains represent. Rich in fiber, vitamins, and minerals, whole grains contribute to a well-balanced diet that supports digestive health and overall well-being. This section provides a comprehensive understanding of the health benefits associated with incorporating diverse whole grains into one's daily meals.

Whole Grains in Everyday Cooking: Practical Integration

Recognizing the importance of practicality, this section offers guidance on seamlessly integrating whole grains into everyday cooking. Whether it's substituting refined grains with their whole counterparts or incorporating ancient grains into familiar dishes, readers are empowered to make small yet impactful changes that align with the principles of anti-inflammatory eating.

From Breakfast to Dinner: Whole Grains at Every Meal

The chapter concludes with a showcase of how whole grains can be enjoyed at every meal, from wholesome breakfast options to satisfying dinner plates. Readers leave with the understanding that whole grains are not just a nutritional necessity but a delightful and accessible addition to their culinary repertoire.

As we wrap up this chapter, readers are equipped with the knowledge and inspiration to embrace the diversity of whole grains, recognizing them not only as a nutritional powerhouse but also as a canvas for culinary creativity in the realm of anti-inflammatory cooking.

Chapter Eight

Advanced Culinary Techniques for Anti-Inflammatory Cooking

Welcome to a chapter that elevates anti-inflammatory cooking to an art form, exploring advanced culinary techniques that not only enhance flavors but also preserve the nutritional integrity of ingredients. Join us as we delve into the world of culinary mastery, where technique meets the principles of anti-inflammatory living.

Mastering Cooking Methods for Nutrient Preservation

The chapter kicks off by emphasizing the importance of cooking methods that preserve the nutrient content of ingredients. From steaming and sautéing to sous-vide and low-temperature cooking, readers are introduced to techniques that go beyond the basics, ensuring that the meals they prepare not only delight the palate but also deliver optimal nutritional benefits.

Sous-Vide and Low-Temperature Cooking: Precision in Flavor

In this section, we take a closer look at sous-vide and low-temperature cooking, exploring how precision in temperature control enhances the flavors, textures, and nutritional profiles of ingredients. Readers gain insights into the art of sous-vide cooking, where ingredients are sealed in a vacuum and slow-cooked to perfection, resulting in tender and succulent dishes that embody anti-inflammatory principles.

Infusing Flavors with Fermentation and Pickling

The chapter unfolds into the world of fermentation and pickling, techniques that not only enhance flavors but also contribute to gut health. From sauerkraut to kimchi and pickled vegetables, readers discover how these methods add depth and complexity to dishes while incorporating gut-friendly probiotics—an additional layer of benefit in the context of anti-inflammatory eating.

Infusing Oils and Creating Flavorful Extracts

A culinary journey wouldn't be complete without exploring the art of infusing oils and creating flavorful extracts. This section provides practical guidance on infusing oils with herbs and spices, allowing readers to craft custom blends that elevate their dishes. Additionally, we delve into creating extracts from ingredients like vanilla and citrus, unlocking a world of concentrated flavors for use in anti-inflammatory cooking.

Creative Plating Techniques: The Visual Feast

Beyond taste, this section explores creative plating techniques that turn meals into visual feasts. From edible flowers to artistic arrangements, readers are guided on how to present their anti-inflammatory creations in a way that not only pleases the eyes but also enhances the overall dining experience.

Balancing Complexity: Making Advanced Techniques Accessible

Recognizing the desire for approachability, the chapter concludes with insights on how to balance advanced techniques with practicality. Tips for planning, prepping, and incorporating these techniques into everyday cooking empower readers to experiment and gradually integrate advanced culinary methods into their anti-inflammatory culinary repertoire.

As we conclude this chapter, readers are equipped with the knowledge and confidence to embark on a culinary adventure that goes beyond the ordinary. Advanced techniques become not just a showcase of skill but a means to fully embrace the principles of anti-inflammatory cooking, ensuring that every meal is a masterpiece of flavor, nutrition, and culinary artistry.

Chapter Nine

Balancing Act - Crafting Well-Balanced Anti-Inflammatory Meals

Welcome to a chapter that goes beyond individual ingredients and explores the art of crafting meals that are not only delicious but also nutritionally balanced. In this balancing act, we delve into the synergy of proteins, fats, and carbohydrates, ensuring that each meal aligns with the principles of an anti-inflammatory diet.

Designing Meals with Proteins, Fats, and Carbohydrates

The chapter opens with an exploration of the fundamental components of well-balanced meals: proteins, fats, and carbohydrates. Readers gain insights into the role of each macronutrient in supporting overall health and are guided on how to create meals that strike the right balance, ensuring sustained energy, satiety, and optimal nutrient absorption.

Protein Variety: Beyond Meat and Plant-Based Alternatives

Diversity takes center stage as we explore the rich tapestry of protein sources. From animal-based options like poultry and fish to plant-based alternatives such as legumes and tofu, readers discover the importance of incorporating a variety of proteins into their meals. This section provides practical tips on balancing different protein sources to create nutritionally complete and satisfying dishes.

The Role of Healthy Fats: Navigating Quantity and Quality

Emphasizing the importance of healthy fats, this section provides guidance on navigating the quantity and quality of fats in a well-balanced diet. Readers learn how to incorporate sources of monounsaturated and polyunsaturated fats, such as avocados and nuts, in proportions that support cardiovascular health and overall well-being.

Navigating Carbohydrates: From Whole Grains to Colorful Vegetables

Carbohydrates take the spotlight as we explore the array of options available, from whole grains to vibrant vegetables. The chapter provides insights into the benefits of choosing complex carbohydrates that provide sustained energy without causing spikes in blood sugar levels. Practical tips on portion control and carbohydrate selection empower readers to make informed choices in crafting anti-inflammatory meals.

Portion Control and Mindful Eating: A Holistic Approach

Recognizing that balance extends beyond individual nutrients, this section delves into the importance of portion control and mindful eating. Readers gain practical strategies for listening to hunger and fullness cues, ensuring that meals are not only nutritionally balanced but also aligned with the principles of anti-inflammatory living.

Meal Timing and Composition: Optimizing Nutrient Absorption

The chapter concludes with considerations for meal timing and composition to optimize nutrient absorption. From pre-workout meals to post-dinner snacks, readers gain insights into how the timing of meals and snacks can impact energy levels, digestion, and overall well-being. Practical guidelines ensure that every aspect of meal planning contributes to the creation of well-balanced, anti-inflammatory meals.

As we wrap up this chapter, readers are empowered to approach meal planning with a holistic perspective, understanding that true balance is achieved not through strict rules but through a thoughtful combination of diverse nutrients. Each meal becomes an opportunity to nourish the body, support overall health, and savor the joys of anti-inflammatory living.

Chapter Ten

Sweet Endings - Desserts with a Health Twist

Welcome to the delectable finale of our anti-inflammatory culinary journey. Chapter 10 is a celebration of sweet endings that not only satisfy the sweet tooth but also align with the principles of health and wellness. Join us as we explore the art of crafting desserts with a health-conscious twist, proving that indulgence and well-being can coexist.

Understanding the Role of Sweeteners in Healthful Desserts

The chapter kicks off by delving into the world of sweeteners, providing insights into natural alternatives that add sweetness without compromising health. From honey and maple syrup to stevia and monk fruit, readers discover options that not only satiate sugar cravings but also contribute additional nutrients and antioxidants to their desserts.

Incorporating Anti-Inflammatory Ingredients into Desserts

Beyond sweeteners, we explore the realm of anti-inflammatory ingredients that can transform desserts into nutritional powerhouses. From antioxidant-rich berries to the warmth of cinnamon and the earthy notes of dark chocolate, readers are guided on how to infuse their sweet creations with ingredients that not only satisfy the palate but also promote total well-being

Creative Flour Alternatives: From Nut Flours to Ancient Grains

This section explores the diverse array of flours that go beyond traditional refined options. Almond flour, coconut flour, and ancient grains like spelt become the canvas for creating desserts that are not only gluten-free but also nutrient-dense. Practical tips on incorporating these alternatives empower readers to experiment with new textures and flavors in their baking.

Reducing Added Sugars: A Practical Approach

Recognizing the impact of added sugars on inflammation, this section offers practical strategies for reducing sugar content in desserts without sacrificing sweetness. Readers gain insights into the art of balancing flavors and utilizing natural sweetness from fruits to create desserts that are both satisfying and health-conscious.

Dessert Recipes That Nourish: A Sweet Culinary Finale

The chapter culminates in a collection of dessert recipes that showcase the versatility of healthful sweet endings. From berry-infused parfaits to nutty energy bites and wholesome fruit sorbets, each recipe is a testament to the creative possibilities of crafting desserts that not only taste divine but also contribute to an anti-inflammatory lifestyle.

Balancing Portion Sizes and Mindful Indulgence

As we approach the end of our culinary journey, the chapter addresses the importance of portion control and mindful indulgence. Practical tips on savoring the sweetness in moderation and appreciating the sensory experience of desserts empower readers to enjoy the pleasures of the table without compromising their commitment to anti-inflammatory living.

This chapter concludes our exploration with a sweet note, proving that the joy of desserts can be seamlessly integrated into a health-conscious lifestyle. With the knowledge gained from Chapter 10, readers can approach sweet endings with a new perspective, reveling in the art of crafting desserts that not only please the palate but also contribute to overall well-being.

Chapter Eleven

Meal Planning and Prep - A Practical Approach

In this pivotal chapter, we shift our focus to the practical aspects of anti-inflammatory living—meal planning and preparation. Chapter 11 serves as a guide, offering practical strategies and efficient techniques to seamlessly incorporate anti-inflammatory principles into daily life. Join us as we explore the art of planning, prepping, and navigating the demands of a busy lifestyle while prioritizing health and well-being.

The Foundation of Anti-Inflammatory Meal
Planning

The chapter opens with an exploration of the
foundational elements of effective meal
planning. Readers gain insights into creating
balanced and diverse menus that align with
anti-inflammatory principles. From
incorporating a variety of colors to ensuring a
mix of macronutrients, this section sets the
stage for practical meal planning that
supports overall health.

Batch Cooking Strategies for Efficiency

Recognizing the time constraints of modern
life, this section dives into the art of batch
cooking. Readers discover strategies for
preparing large quantities of

anti-inflammatory staples, such as grains, proteins, and vegetables, in advance. Practical tips on storage and creative ways to repurpose batch-cooked components empower individuals to streamline their cooking process without compromising variety or flavor.

Strategic Ingredient Selection for Versatile Meals

The chapter unfolds into the strategic selection of versatile ingredients that can be used across multiple meals. From preparing a large batch of a versatile sauce to incorporating ingredients that serve as building blocks for various dishes, readers gain insights into creating a repertoire of components that simplify meal preparation while maintaining culinary diversity.

Weekly and Monthly Meal Planning Guides

Practical meal planning guides are presented, offering readers customizable templates for weekly and monthly meal planning. These guides provide structure while allowing flexibility, enabling individuals to adapt their plans based on personal preferences, dietary needs, and the ever-changing demands of life.

Efficient Grocery Shopping for Anti-Inflammatory Living

Navigating the grocery store with a focus on anti-inflammatory ingredients becomes an essential skill explored in this section.

Readers gain practical tips for creating shopping lists, choosing fresh and seasonal produce, and navigating the aisles with an informed eye for selecting nutrient-dense, anti-inflammatory foods.

Mindful Eating Practices for Lasting Habits

Recognizing that meal planning extends beyond the kitchen, this section delves into mindful eating practices. From savoring each bite to being attuned to hunger and fullness cues, readers discover how incorporating mindfulness into their eating habits complements the overall anti-inflammatory lifestyle.

Adapting Meal Plans to Special Dietary Needs

Acknowledging the diverse dietary needs of individuals, this section provides guidance on adapting meal plans to accommodate various preferences and restrictions. Whether following specific diets like gluten-free or vegan, or catering to food allergies, readers gain insights into creating customized meal plans that prioritize health without sacrificing taste or satisfaction.

As we conclude Chapter 11, readers are armed with practical tools and a holistic approach to meal planning and preparation. This chapter empowers individuals to seamlessly integrate anti-inflammatory principles into their daily lives, fostering sustainable habits that prioritize health without compromising the joy of nourishing, flavorful meals.

Chapter Twelve

Navigating Social and Dining Out Challenges

In this chapter, we tackle the social and dining out aspects of anti-inflammatory living, recognizing that life's celebrations and gatherings often revolve around shared meals. Chapter 12 serves as a guide to navigating social events, restaurant outings, and special occasions while staying true to anti-inflammatory principles. Join us as we explore strategies to maintain balance and make informed choices in a variety of social settings.

Anti-Inflammatory Principles in Social Settings

The chapter opens with a discussion on applying anti-inflammatory principles in social settings. Readers gain insights into making mindful choices without feeling restricted, whether at a friend's dinner party, a family gathering, or a celebratory event. The focus is on striking a balance between enjoying the occasion and adhering to anti-inflammatory goals.

Strategies for Healthy Choices at Restaurants

Navigating restaurant menus can be a challenge, but this section offers practical strategies for making healthful choices while dining out. From deciphering menu descriptions to requesting modifications, readers gain insights into selecting dishes that align with anti-inflammatory principles without sacrificing the pleasure of a restaurant experience.

Anticipating Challenges and Planning Ahead

Anticipating challenges in social and dining out scenarios is key to success. This section provides readers with proactive strategies for planning ahead, such as reviewing menus before arriving at a restaurant, communicating dietary preferences with hosts, and bringing a dish to share that aligns with anti-inflammatory principles.

Mindful Eating in Social Settings

Mindful eating practices take center stage as we explore techniques for staying present and savoring the flavors in social settings. From pacing oneself during a meal to engaging in conversation between bites, readers gain tools for making mindful choices that contribute to both enjoyment and well-being.

Celebrating Special Occasions Mindfully

Special occasions often involve indulgent foods, and this section guides readers on how to celebrate without compromising anti-inflammatory goals. Whether it's a birthday, holiday, or festive gathering, readers learn to make thoughtful choices that honor the occasion while prioritizing health.

Handling Peer Pressure and Naysayers

Social situations can sometimes involve peer pressure or encounters with naysayers. This section provides strategies for gracefully handling situations where others may question or challenge anti-inflammatory choices. Readers gain confidence in their decisions and learn to navigate social dynamics with resilience and tact.

Balancing Flexibility and Consistency

Recognizing that life is a dynamic interplay of various commitments and pleasures, this section explores the delicate balance between flexibility and consistency. Readers discover how to adapt to different situations while maintaining a core commitment to anti-inflammatory living, ensuring that health-conscious choices become an integrated part of their lifestyle.

Strategies for Alcohol Consumption in Social Settings

Addressing a common element of social gatherings, this section provides insights into navigating alcohol consumption in a health-conscious way. From choosing lower-inflammatory beverages to moderating intake, readers gain practical tips for maintaining balance while participating in social events.

As we conclude Chapter 12, readers are equipped with a comprehensive toolkit for successfully navigating social and dining out challenges. This chapter reinforces the idea that anti-inflammatory living is not about deprivation but rather making informed choices that prioritize health while still enjoying the rich tapestry of social and culinary experiences life has to offers.

www.ingramcontent.com/pod-product-compliance
Lightning Source LLC
Chambersburg PA
CBHW062237290526
45794CB00006B/2318